# Kid's Box

**Updated Second Edition**

Student's Book 3

American English

Caroline Nixon & Michael Tomlinson

# Language summary

| | Key vocabulary | Key grammar and functions | Phonics |
|---|---|---|---|
| **Hello!** page 4 | Character names<br>Numbers: *1–20*<br>Colors: *black, blue, gray, green, orange, pink, purple, red, white, yellow*<br>Toys: *bike, camera, computer, doll, game, helicopter, kite, monster, train, truck* | Greetings: Hello. What's your name? My name's … How old are you? I'm (eight). I like (reading). What's her/his name? His name's … / It's called … , Have<br>Present progressive for present actions<br>Prepositions: *next to, on, in front of, under, between, behind*<br>Can for ability | Rhyming words |
| **1 Family matters** page 10 | Family: *aunt, uncle, daughter, son, granddaughter, grandson, parents, grandparents*<br>Describing people: *beard, curly/fair/straight hair, smart, mustache, naughty, quiet* | Possessive 's<br>Present progressive for present actions<br>Simple present<br>Like, love, enjoy + -ing / nouns, want + infinitive<br>Short answers Yes, I do. / No, I don't. | Long vowel sound "ay" (b*ay*by) and sound "ar" (*ar*tist) |
| Art Portraits page 16 | | | |
| **2 Home sweet home** page 18 | Numbers: *21–100*<br>Houses: *apartment, balcony, basement, downstairs, elevator, stairs, upstairs*<br>Places: *city, town, country* | What's your address? It's … .<br>Present progressive for present actions<br>Prepositions: *above, below*<br>need<br>Have | Long vowel sound "oa" (g*oa*t) and vowel sound "ou" (cl*ow*n) |
| Geography Homes page 24 | | Review 1 and 2 page 26 | |
| **3 A day in the life** page 28 | Routines: *catch the bus, do homework, get dressed, get undressed, get up, go to bed/school, put on, take a shower, take off, wake up, wash*<br>*before, after*<br>*seven o'clock*<br>Days of the week | Simple present for routines: statements and questions<br>How often … ?<br>Frequency adverbs: *always, sometimes, never, every day* | Long vowel sound: "or" (h*or*se) |
| Science The heart page 34 | | | |
| **4 In the city** page 36 | In town: *bank, bus station, hospital, library, market, movie theater, parking lot, sports center, store, supermarket, swimming pool* | Prepositions: *close to, across from*<br>Where's the … ?<br>Infinitives of purpose: *You go there to buy food.*<br>Must for obligation<br>Impersonal *you*<br>Can for permission | Consonant sound: "s" (*c*ity, i*c*e) |
| Math Counting money page 42 | | Review 3 and 4 page 44 | |

| | | Key vocabulary | Key grammar and functions | Phonics |
|---|---|---|---|---|
| 5 | Stay healthy<br>page 46 | Illness: *a backache, a cold, a cough, an earache, a headache, a stomachache, a temperature, a toothache* | What's the matter (with you/him/her/them)?<br>I/They have, He/She has …<br>My … hurts.<br>I'm not very well.<br>Positive and negative obligations: *must/must not*<br>Permission and ability: *can/can't* | Rhyming words |
| | Science — A healthy body | page 52 | | |
| 6 | A day in the country<br>page 54 | In the country: *field, forest, grass, lake, leaf, picnic, plant, river*<br>Adjectives: *bad, cold, fat, hot, hungry, loud, quiet, strong, thin, thirsty, tired, weak* | Suggestions and offers: *Should I … ?* | Short vowel sound: "e" (h<u>ea</u>d) and long vowel sound: "ee" (<u>ea</u>t) |
| | Science — Plants | page 60 | Review 5 and 6 — page 62 | |
| 7 | World of animals<br>page 64 | Animals: *bat, bear, dolphin, kangaroo, lion, panda, parrot, shark, whale* | Comparative of common irregular and one- and two-syllable regular adjectives: *bad / worse, good / bad, -y, -ier, -er*<br>Doubling of consonants: *thin / thinner* | Consonant sound: "f" (dol<u>ph</u>in) |
| | Geography — Animal habitats | page 70 | | |
| 8 | Weather report<br>page 72 | Weather: *cloudy, cold, dry, hot, rain, rainbow, raining, rainy, snow, snowing*<br>*coat, scarf, sweater* | What's the weather like (at the beach)?<br>It's …<br>Simple past: *was/wasn't, were/weren't* | Consonant sound: "w" (<u>w</u>hy, <u>w</u>ere) |

Music — Instruments — page 78

Review 7 and 8 — page 80

Values 1 & 2 — Give and share — page 82

Values 5 & 6 — Fair play — page 84

Values 3 & 4 — Love your city — page 83

Values 7 & 8 — Help the world — page 85

Grammar reference — page 86

# Hello!

**1** Read and say the name.

**a** Hello. I'm nine. I have a brother and a sister. This is my favorite computer game. It's called "Brainbox."

**b** Hello. I'm five. I have a big dog. She's black and white, and her name's Dotty.

**c** Hi. I'm eight. I like reading comic books. My favorite comic book's called "Lock and Key."

Scott     Sally     Suzy

**2** Listen and check.

**3** Ask and answer.
1. What's your name?   *My name's …*
2. How old are you?
3. Do you have a brother or a sister?
4. What's your favorite toy called?

## LOOK

My favorite comic book's **called** "Lock and Key."

**4** 🎧 **Listen. Say the number and the color.**

D-O-L-L

Doll. That's number eighteen, and it's pink.

**5** **Play the game.**

B-I-K-E

Bike. That's number seventeen, and it's purple.

**6** **Read and answer.**
1 It's on the table, next to the books.   Computer.
2 It's on the box, next to the ball.
3 It's on the floor, in front of the train.
4 It's under the table.
5 It's on the floor, between the helicopter and the monster.

**7** Read and match the names.  〔Eva – c〕

Scott and Sally are in the playground with their friends Alex, Robert, and Eva and their sister, Suzy. Eva's sitting next to Sally, and Scott's talking to Robert. Alex is behind them.

**8** 🔊 **Listen. Who is it?**

〔She's drinking orange juice.〕  〔That's Eva.〕

**9** Answer the questions.
1 What's Sally doing?  〔She's reading.〕
2 What's Alex doing?
3 What's Robert eating?
4 What's Suzy doing?
5 What's Eva drinking?
6 What's Scott doing?
7 What's Alex kicking?
8 What's Sally reading?

🔍 **LOOK**
What**'s** Suzy doing?   What **is** Suzy doing?
She**'s** jumping.   She **is** jumping.

**10** 🔊 Listen and say the name.

I have an old bike,
And I'm riding it.
He has a big kite,
And he's flying it.
She has a small car,
And she's driving it.
We have toys!

I have a big doll,
And it's talking.
He has a robot,
And it's walking.
She has a new ball,
And it's bouncing.
We have toys!

Mary
Vicky
Jim
Fred
Oh, no!
I'm happy.
Stacey
Paul

**11** 🔊 Sing the song.

**12** Look, read, and write.
Complete the sentences.
1 Jim is flying a big _____ .
2 Stacey is carrying a fat _____ .

Answer the questions.
3 What does Paul have?
4 What is Mary doing?
5 Write two sentences about the picture.

## 13 Sally's phonics

**Hello / Head / Clean** — Jim

**Yellow / Red / Green** — Kim

Jim and Kim are playing a game.

They're saying words that sound the same.

## 14 Ask and answer.

ride a bike   play badminton   swim   play the piano   sing   play soccer

Can you play soccer?
Yes, I can.

Can you swim?
No, I can't.

# LOCK & KEY

**Hello. This is the Lock and Key Detective Agency. Sorry we can't answer the phone right now. Please leave a message.**

**Please help me! I'm in the house next to your agency. I can't find Clarence!**

**Argh! Oops! Hello, hello. This is Key. Can I help you?**

**Oh! Please find Clarence. He's a big fat cat. He has long white fur and blue eyes. He doesn't have a tail.**

TRIP!

**Get the Detective Box, Key. We have work to do!**

**Come on, Key. What are we looking for?**

**We're looking for a big white cat, Lock. No problem.**

# 1 Family matters

**1** Look, think, and answer.
1. Is Sally at school?
2. Who's on the poster?
3. Does she have a brother?
4. How many sisters does she have?

My family tree.

aunt   daughter   granddaughter   grandson   grandparents   parents   son   uncle

**2** Listen and check.

**3** Ask and answer.
1. Who's Sally's uncle?   Uncle Fred.
2. Who's Suzy's aunt?
3. Who are Scott's grandparents?
4. Who are Mrs. Star's daughters?
5. Who's Mr. Star's son?
6. Who's Grandpa Star's grandson?

**LOOK**
Who's Sally's uncle?
Who is Sally's uncle?

**4** **Listen and say the letter.**

He's taking a picture of his son.

e

**5** **Listen and complete.**

Suzy's sitting next to her …

mom.

**6** **Ask and answer.**

Who's playing a game with her aunt?

Sally.

playing a game    reading    playing soccer    painting    taking a picture

**7** Look, think, and answer.
1. Where's Sally?
2. Is Scott happy?
3. Is Dotty naughty?
4. Who's painting?

**8** Read and check.

Hi! I'm Aunt May.

Look at everyone in the yard! Sally's reading. She enjoys reading about science. She's smart, and she wants to be a doctor. Scott's wearing his helmet because he's riding his bike. He's with his Uncle Fred. They love riding bikes.

Suzy wants to give her dog a bath. Dotty's naughty. She doesn't like taking baths. Grandpa's standing next to the bathtub, and he needs a towel.

Grandma's quiet. She enjoys painting. She's painting a beautiful picture of her granddaughter, Sally.

**9** Say "yes" or "no."
1. Scott doesn't enjoy riding his bike.
2. Sally enjoys reading about science.
3. Scott doesn't wear a helmet.
4. Suzy wants to give her doll a bath.
5. Dotty likes taking baths.
6. Grandma enjoys painting.

**LOOK**

Scott **enjoys riding** his bike.   Scott **wants to ride** his bike.

**10** **Complete the song with the names. Then listen and check.**

Aunt May's a doctor,
She has straight black hair.
_____'s a farmer,
His beard is short and fair.

_____ is quiet,
She wants to paint all day.
_____ is funny,
And his curly hair is gray.

_____ can be naughty,
He loves "Lock and Key."
His sister _____'s smart,
And she doesn't like TV.

_____ isn't quiet,
But she's very small.
Here's our family,
We really love them all.
We really love them all.

**11** **Sing the song.**

**12** **Draw your family tree. Talk about your family. Use the words in the boxes.**

| She's He's | my | aunt. uncle. grandmother. grandfather. |
|---|---|---|

| She's He's | my | father's mother's grandmother's grandfather's | brother. sister. son. daughter. |
|---|---|---|---|

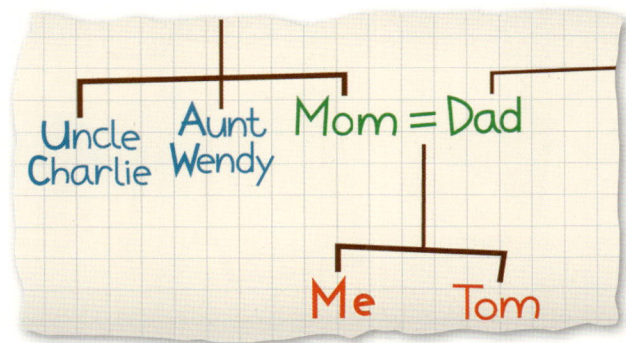

Uncle Charlie   Aunt Wendy   Mom = Dad
                              Me   Tom

## 13 Sally's phonics

Mark's an artist.

Jane's a baby.

Mark's painting Jane in the yard.

## 14 Ask and answer. Use the words in the box.

Do you like playing on your laptop?   Yes, I do.

listening   playing   riding   watching   wearing   eating   drinking

## 15 Write about your friend's answers. Tell the class.

Jack likes eating fruit. He doesn't like drinking milk.
He likes playing basketball. He doesn't like playing on his laptop.

# LOCK & KEY

**Hmmm, that's the pet thief. He has straight black hair, a black beard, and a mustache.**

**WANTED Pet Thief**

**Yes, and he's wearing a big dirty hat and an old jacket. We can find him, no problem!**

**Where are you going, Lock?**

**I want to find that pet thief. Let's look in the park.**

**Look! There's the pet thief ... and he has Clarence!**

**Yes, I can see his dirty hat and old jacket.**

**Let's get him!**

**There you are Clarence! Naughty cat!**

**What are you doing? Give me my cat! Who are you?**

**I'm Mr. Key, from Lock and Key Detective Agency. We're looking for the pet thief.**

**I'm not a pet thief!**

**That's right, Key. She doesn't have a beard or a mustache. Give her the cat.**

**No problem, Lock.**

## Art | Portraits

**Fact:** Oil paintings can take many years to dry.

**1** Read, look, and answer.

Look at these two pictures. Which one is a portrait?

There are a lot of different types of paintings. A picture of a person or a group of people is called a portrait. A painting of the artist is called a self-portrait.

**2** 🔊 CD1 22 Look at the self-portraits. Listen and say the letter.

a   b    c    d 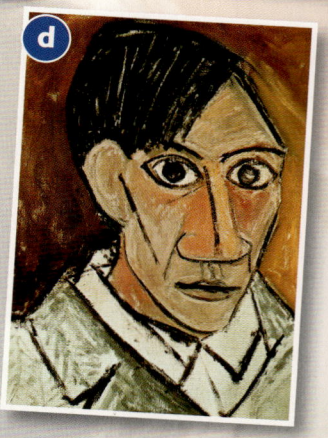   e

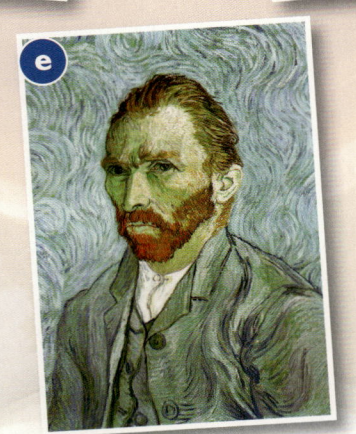

## 3 Look at the family portraits. Look and find.
1 A woman in a purple dress.
2 A man with a red hat.
3 A black cat.
4 Two men with gray hair.

a   b    c    d

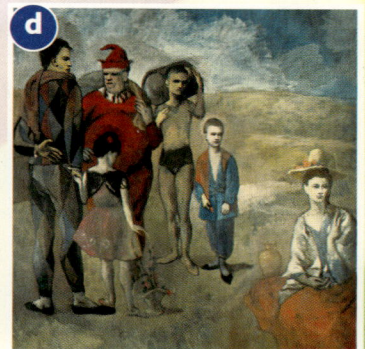

## 4 Now match the texts with the portraits.

1 I love this portrait by Ursula Roma. It has a lot of colors. We can see the family and their pets.

2 This is my favorite family portrait. It's by Pablo Picasso. I can see three children with their parents and grandfather.

3 I love old paintings. I like this portrait by Copley. It's very old, and we can see his family. He has four children.

4 The parents are both wearing hats. They are walking with their son and daughter. I love this portrait by Hulis Mavruk because it's very happy.

**Project** Draw your family portrait.

# 2 Home sweet home

**1** Look, think, and answer.
1. What buildings can you see?
2. What's in the room under the house?
3. Where's the apartment?
4. Does the apartment have a yard?

- upstairs
- downstairs
- elevator
- balcony
- stairs
- basement
- A house in the country
- An apartment downtown

**2** Listen and check.

**3** Listen and say the letter.

**4** 🔊 Listen and order. 1 – c

**a**
Upstairs, downstairs,
One floor or two.
We live here,
What about you?

**b**
Home is home … ,
In an apartment or a house,
In a city or the country.
Home is home!
It's where I'm free.

**c**
We have a basement
Under the ground floor.
It has brown stairs
And a purple door.

**d**
I have an elevator,
It goes up and down.
From my balcony,
I can see the town.

**5** 🔊 Sing the song.

**6** Talk to your friend. Are your houses the same or different?

- I live in a town.
- Same! I live in a town.
- My house has three bedrooms.
- Different! My house doesn't have three bedrooms.

**7** Look, read, and match.   1 – f

**Eva moves to a new apartment.**

a b c
d e f

1. Today Eva and her family are moving. Two men are carrying the couch to the moving truck.

2. Her new address is 14 Park Road. It's an apartment.

3. There's an elevator, but it's very small. The men can't take the couch in the elevator. They need to carry it up the stairs.

4. Eva's helping. She's taking a lamp upstairs. She's smiling because she can go in the elevator.

5. The men are climbing the stairs with the couch. It's difficult to carry.

6. Now the men are sitting on the couch. They're taking a break. They need a cold drink.

**8** Write some words to complete the sentences about the story. You can use 1, 2, or 3 words.

1 Eva and her family  are moving  today.
2 The two men are putting the couch in _____.
3 Eva's new apartment is on _____.
4 Eva's carrying a _____ in the elevator.
5 The men need to carry _____ upstairs because the elevator is very small.
6 The men are _____ because they are hot, tired, and thirsty.

**9** Listen and say.

12  13  14  15  16  17  18  19  100
20  30  40  50  60  70  80  90

**10** Listen. What color are the doors?

"May lives at number 72."  "That's pink."

**11** Ask and answer.

"What number's the yellow door?"  "It's number twenty-three."

**12** Talk about where you live.

"What's your address?"  "It's 72 Station Road."

🔍 **LOOK**

| thirteen | thirty | seventeen | seventy |
| fourteen | forty | eighteen | eighty |
| fifteen | fifty | nineteen | ninety |
| sixteen | sixty | | one hundred |

## 13 Sally's phonics

A goat in a yellow coat …

and a clown with a flower in his mouth.

## 14 Ask and answer.

What's your name?   Where do you live?
What's your address?   What's your phone number?

| Name | | | | |
|---|---|---|---|---|
| Address | | | | |
| Place | | | | |
| Phone number | | | | |

# LOCK & KEY

**Beautiful house, Mrs. Potts. It's very old.**

**I think it has a monster.**

**It lives under the stairs in the basement. It comes upstairs at night.**

**Oh, I don't think so, Mrs. Potts. There are no monsters.**

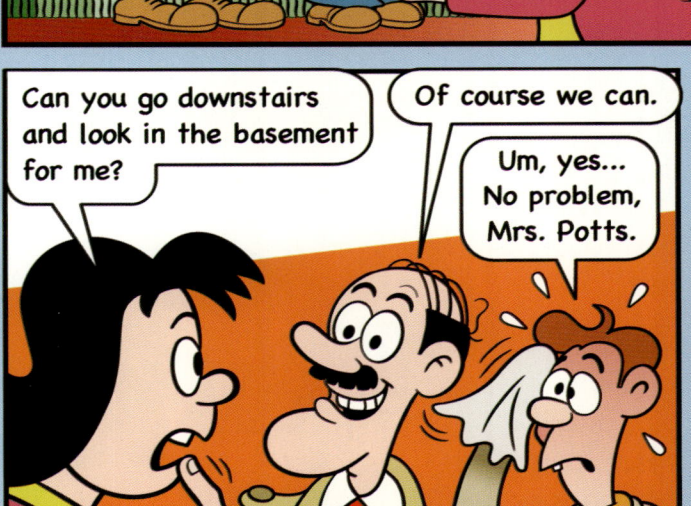

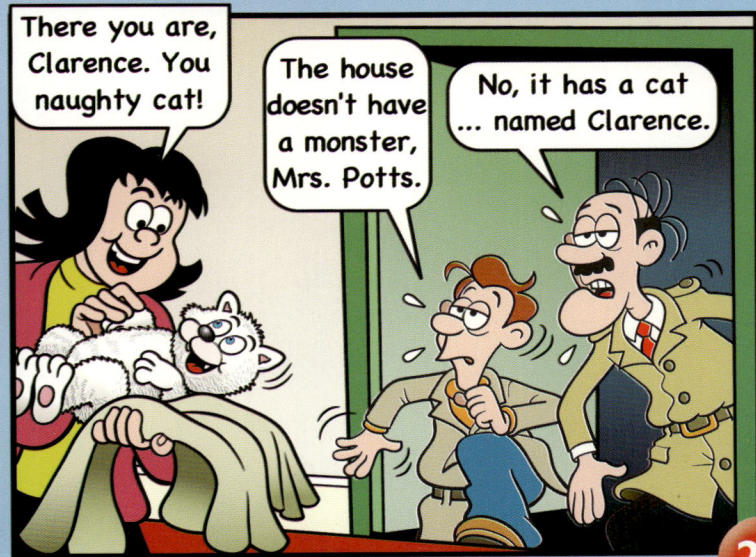

**Can you go downstairs and look in the basement for me?**

**Of course we can.**

**Um, yes... No problem, Mrs. Potts.**

**I'm not happy about this, Lock. I don't like it.**

**Aagghhh!**

**YOWL!**

**It's a monster!**

**There you are, Clarence. You naughty cat!**

**The house doesn't have a monster, Mrs. Potts.**

**No, it has a cat ... named Clarence.**

# Geography — Homes

**Fact:** Half the people in the world live in cities.

### 1 🔊 Read, listen, and match.

a. Vicky

b. Jack

c. Peter

d. Daisy

1. I live in a small apartment in the city. The kitchen and the living room are one room. I love living in the center of the city.

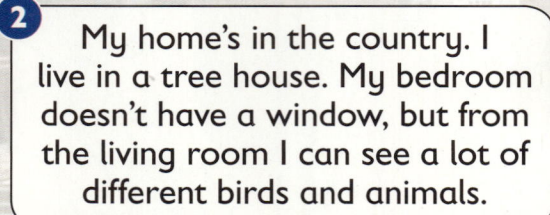

2. My home's in the country. I live in a tree house. My bedroom doesn't have a window, but from the living room I can see a lot of different birds and animals.

3. My home is on water. I live in a houseboat. It doesn't have a yard, but I can see ducks from my bedroom! There aren't any streets or roads close to my house. It's great.

4. I live in a castle. My home is very big and very old, and it has fifteen bedrooms. I love walking in the yard because there are a lot of trees.

### 2 Listen, read, and write.

Jack's home: a 1 _____ in the center of the city
the 2 _____ and _____ are in one big room

Vicky's home: a 3 _____ on the water
4 _____ close to her home

Daisy's home: a 5 _____ in the country
a lot of 6 _____ and _____ live close to her home

Peter's home: an old 7 _____
has 8 _____ bedrooms

**3** Ask and answer.

yard   elevator   stores
trees   flowers   big
cars   birds   small
trucks   streets

Where would you like to live?
I'd like to live in a castle.
Why?
Because it has a big yard.

**4** Look at the picture and complete the text.

This is a picture of my dream house. There are three bedrooms upstairs. My bedroom has a small balcony for my _____. In my bedroom there's a big _____. There's an elevator between my bedroom and the _____. This is for my _____. In the big yard next to the house, there is a _____, and there are two _____ to jump on. There's also a fantastic amusement park next to my house. I like my dream house a lot.

**Project**  Draw, label, and write about your dream house.

# Review Units 1 and 2

**1** Play the game.

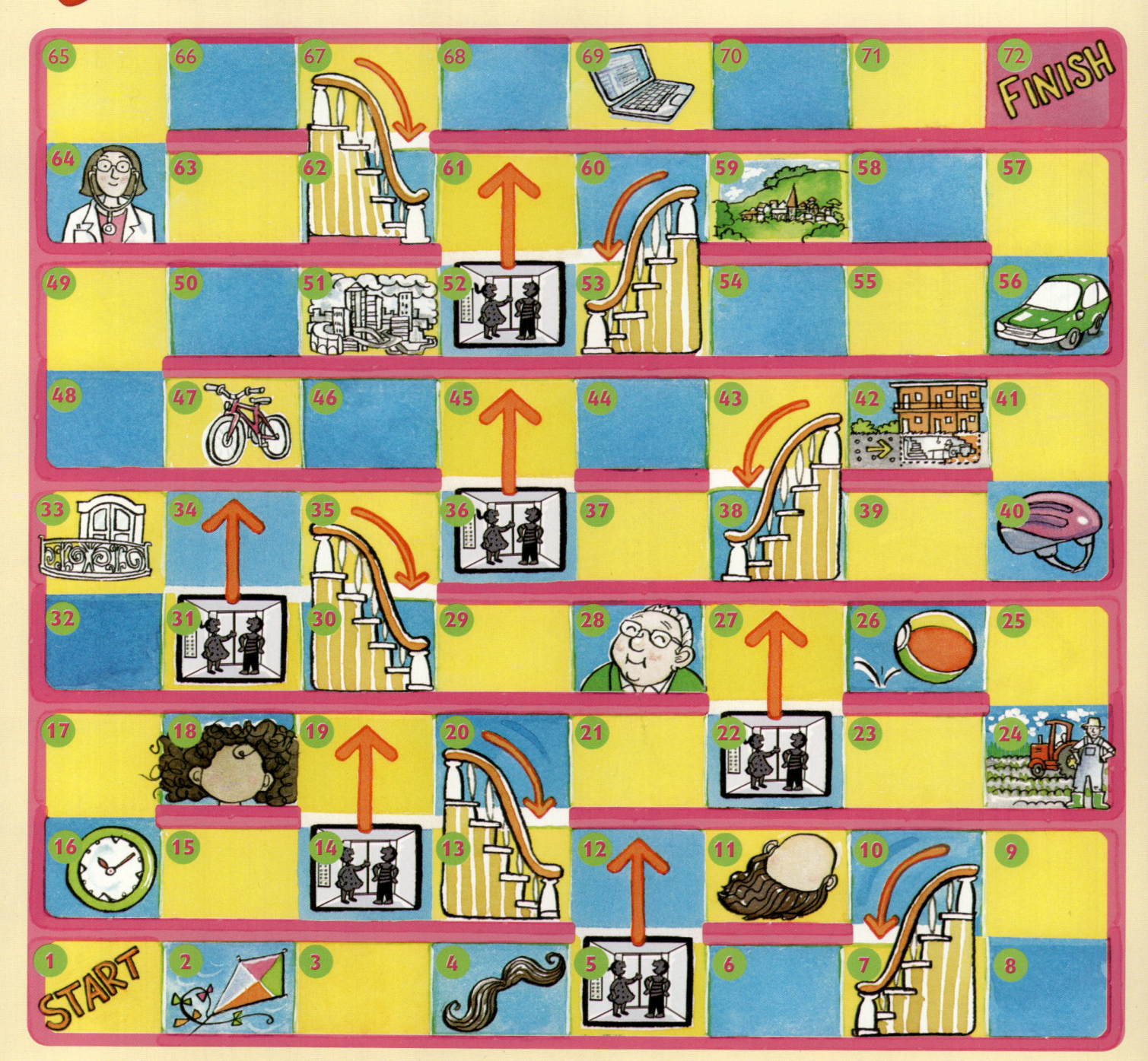

**Instructions**
Elevators – Go up.
Stairs – Go down.
Pictures – Spell the words. If it's right, roll again. If it's wrong, stop.

## 2 Look, read, and write.

**Complete the sentences.**
1 The men are carrying a _____.
2 The girl's carrying a _____ upstairs.

**Answer the questions.**
3 Which room is the family in? _____.
4 What is the boy reading? _____.
5 Write two sentences.

## 3 Look at the pictures. Say which is different.

Picture d is different. She has short hair.

## Quiz!

1 What's Sally's aunt's name?
2 What does Scott's grandmother love doing?
3 What color is Mrs. Potts' cat?
4 Where can you find a basement?
5 What's Eva's new address?
6 Is the pet thief's hair straight or curly?

# 3 A day in the life

**1** 🔊 35 CD1 Listen and say the letter.

a b c
d e f
g h i

get dressed   get undressed   get up   go to bed   take a shower
put on   wake up   take off   wash   catch the bus   do homework

**2** Read and match the sentences to the pictures in Activity 1.

**1** Sally wakes up at seven o'clock every day. **2** Then she gets up. **3** Before breakfast she takes a shower. **4** She gets dressed and puts on her T-shirt and her skirt. **5** At eight o'clock she catches the bus to school. **6** After school Sally does her homework. **7** She washes her hands before dinner. **8** Before bedtime Sally gets undressed and takes off her T-shirt and skirt. **9** She goes to bed at 9 o'clock.

**3** 🔊 36 CD1 Listen and do the actions.

**LOOK**

She wakes up **at** seven **o'clock**.

**4** **Listen and match.** 1 – b

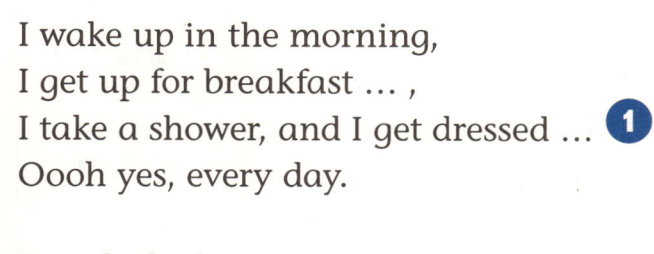

I wake up in the morning,
I get up for breakfast … ,
I take a shower, and I get dressed … ①
Oooh yes, every day.

I catch the bus
to take me to school …
I do my homework on the way … ②
Oooh yes, every day.

Classes start and
I see my teacher … ③
Eleven o'clock and we're out to play … ④
Oooh yes, every day.

I wash my hands ⑤
Before I have my dinner …
I get undressed, and I go to bed … ⑥
Oooh yes, Oooh yes,
Oooh yes, every day, every day …

**5** **Sing the song.**

**6** **Answer the questions.**
1 What time does he get dressed?
2 What time does he do his homework?
3 What time does he start school?
4 What time does he go out to play?
5 What time does he go to bed?

He gets dressed at seven o'clock.

**7** **Ask and answer.**

What do you do before breakfast?

I take a shower.

| What do you do | before / after | breakfast? lunch? dinner? school? bedtime? |
|---|---|---|

29

**8** 🔊 Say the chant.

| SUNDAY | MONDAY | TUESDAY | WEDNESDAY | THURSDAY | FRIDAY | SATURDAY |
|--------|--------|---------|-----------|----------|--------|----------|
|        |        |         |           |          |        |          |

**9** 🔊 Listen and say the day.

a  b  c

**10** 🔊 Listen again. Choose the right words.

1 Scott always / never plays in the park on Mondays.
2 Scott always / sometimes does his homework on Mondays.
3 Scott sometimes / never goes swimming on Wednesdays.
4 Scott always / never plays in the park on Sundays.

1 Scott never plays in the park on Mondays.

**LOOK**

| always | ✓ ✓ ✓ |
| sometimes | ✓ |
| never | ✗ |

30

**11** Look, read, and complete the text.

James Flunk is a music teacher. At school he _____ plays the piano, but he _____ plays the piano on vacation.

James loves playing tennis, so he _____ plays on Wednesdays. He _____ plays soccer with his daughter Jane, too. She _____ scores a goal.

Every Saturday morning James takes his son for his swimming lesson, but James _____ goes swimming.

He sometimes takes his family to the mountains on Sundays. They _____ sing songs in the car.

**12** Listen and say "yes" or "no."

**13** Look and make sentences. Use the words in the boxes.

"I never ride my bike on Mondays."

always   never   sometimes

on Saturdays   on Wednesdays
after school   in the morning

## 14 Sally's phonics

A h**or**se

A st**ory**

A h**or**se reading a st**ory** at f**our** in the m**or**ning.

## 15 Ask and answer.

How often do you watch TV?

Every day.

every day   sometimes   never

1  How often do you watch TV?
2  How often do you eat fruit?
3  How often do you go shopping?
4  How often do you go swimming?
5  How often do you listen to the radio?
6  How often do you play tennis?
7  How often do you read comic books?
8  How often do you ride a bike?

# LOCK & KEY

**Good morning. I'm Johnny Talkalot. On today's show we have the detectives Lock and Key to tell us about their work. We all know detectives work a lot and get up before you and me.**

**Mr. Key, this is Johnny Talkalot. It's nine o'clock! Where are you? You aren't in the detective agency.**

**Oh, no, we never get up before ten o'clock.**

**Everybody knows detectives are very smart.**

**Yes, sometimes we follow people. We're very quiet so they never know we're behind them.**

**YEEOWW! My nose!**

**So, girls and boys, what do you think? Do these detectives work a lot? Are they quiet? And are they very smart?**

33

## Science | The heart

**Fact**
The heart never stops beating.

**1** 🎧 Listen and say "quick" or "slow."

**2** Read and do.

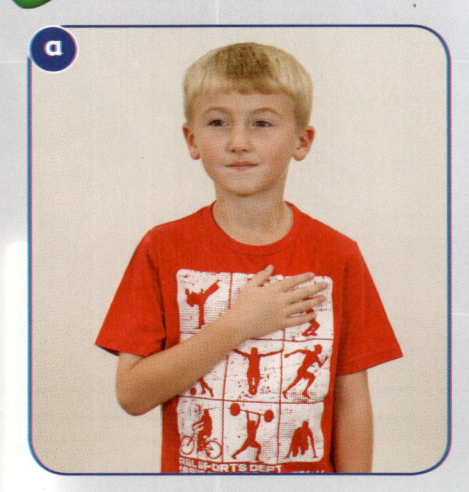

a. Put your hand on your heart. Is your heartbeat quick or slow?

b. Jump up and down for one minute.

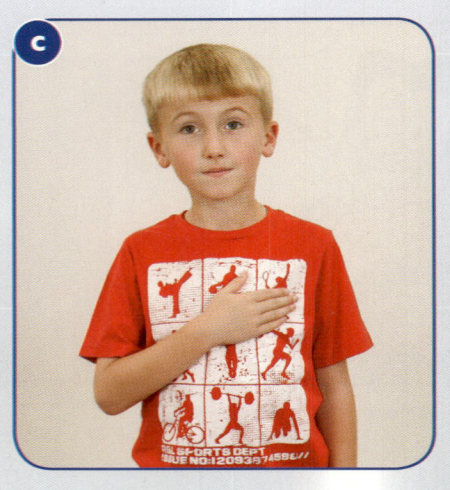

c. Put your hand on your heart again. Is your heartbeat quick or slow?

**3** Read and say "yes" or "no."

Your heart moves the blood in your body. Blood picks up oxygen and sends it to different parts of your body. When you play sports, your heartbeat is quick because your body needs more oxygen.

- blood from the body
- blood to the body
- blood to the lungs
- oxygen
- The heart

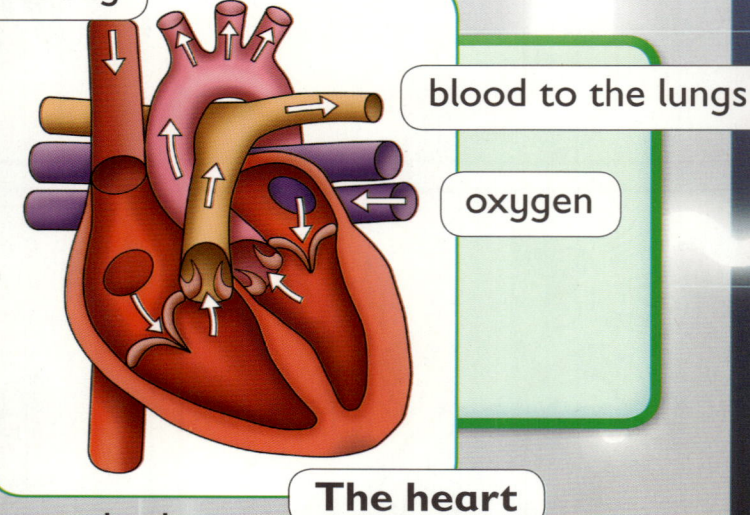

1. Your heart moves the water in your body.
2. Your heart sends oxygen to different parts of your body.
3. Your heartbeat is quick when you are sleeping.
4. Your heartbeat is quick because your body needs more food.

**4** Read, look, and answer.

What do you think?
Quick or slow?

When your heartbeat is slow, your pulse is slow. When your heartbeat is quick, your pulse is quick. Your pulse is the number of heartbeats you have in a minute.

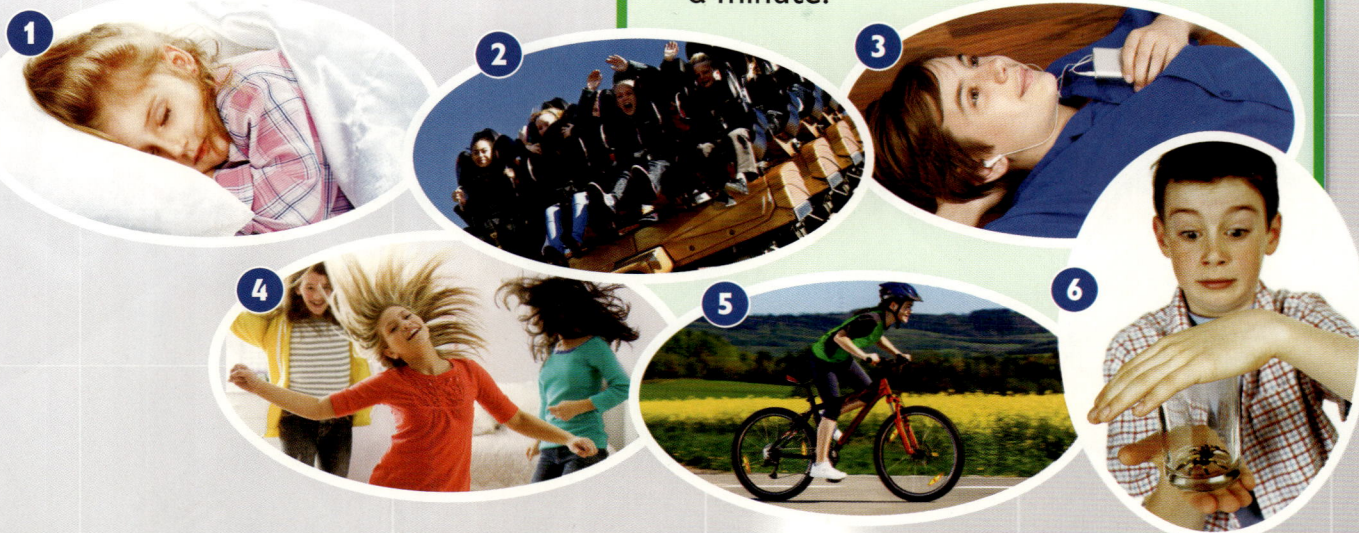

**5** Take your pulse.

Put two fingers on your arm next to your hand. Count the number of heartbeats in a minute.

**Project** Make your pulse chart.

# 4 In the city

**1** 🔊 Listen. Find Eva's apartment.

bank   bus station   movie theater   sports center
supermarket   swimming pool   library   market

**2** Ask and answer.

(What's across from the movie theater?)   (The bus station.)

in front of   behind   next to   between   across from

**3** **Look at the picture. Listen and answer.**

Where's the park?

It's in front of the swimming pool.

**4** **Ask and answer.**
1. Where do you go to see a movie?
2. Where do you go to play badminton?
3. Where do you go to buy food?
4. Where do you go to park a car?
5. Where do you go to catch a bus?
6. Where do you go to see a doctor?
7. Where do you go to fly a kite?
8. Where do you wear a swimsuit?

You go to the movie theater to see a movie.

**5** **Look at the picture. Ask and answer.**

Where's the sports center?

It's next to the swimming pool.

Where's the … ?

It's …

## 6 Look, think, and answer.
1. Where are the children?
2. Which children are happy?
3. What book does Robert have?
4. What time is it?

## 7 Listen and check.

## 8 Listen and say "yes" or "no."

**LOOK**

We **must** be quiet in the library.

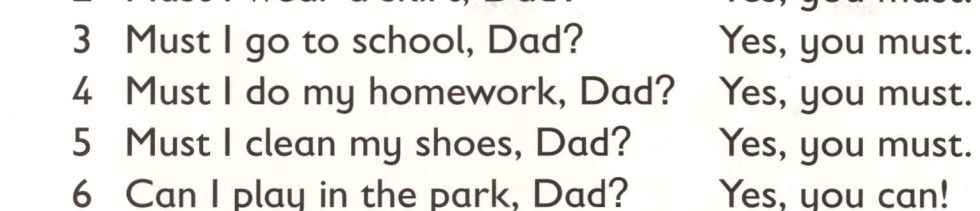

**9**  Read and match. Then listen and check.

1 Must I make my bed, Dad?     Yes, you must.    1 – d
2 Must I wear a skirt, Dad?     Yes, you must.
3 Must I go to school, Dad?     Yes, you must.
4 Must I do my homework, Dad?     Yes, you must.
5 Must I clean my shoes, Dad?     Yes, you must.
6 Can I play in the park, Dad?     Yes, you can!

**10**  Sing the song.

**11** **Sally's phonics**

Cindy and Lucy leave the city.

They go to the circus and eat ice cream.

"This is exciting!" says Cindy.

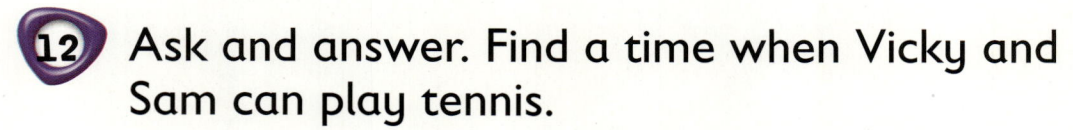

**12** Ask and answer. Find a time when Vicky and Sam can play tennis.

Can Sam play tennis on Friday?

No, he must go to the doctor on Friday.

# LOCK & KEY

Lock and Key are looking for work on the computer.

**Hmm, Lottie Cash, the bank robber. We can find her.**

WANTED — Lottie Cash

**No problem, Lock!**

**I need some money. I must go to the bank.**

**Today is a great day for shopping in the city.**

**Come on then, let's go. I love shopping.**

**It's her! It's Lottie Cash, the bank robber! She's going to the bank now.**

**We must stop her! We need to get there before her.**

**Give me that money, Lottie Cash!**

**Lottie who?**

**Don't touch her money!**

**What? Not you again, Mr. Key!**

**Stand up, Key. You and I need to talk!**

**No problem, Lock!**

# Math  Counting money

**Fact**
Coins can be different shapes. Some coins in Denmark have holes in the middle.

**1** Read. Say and answer.
Look at this money.

What's a? — fifty cents.

In the United States, people use dollars and cents to pay for things. There are one hundred cents (¢) in a dollar ($).

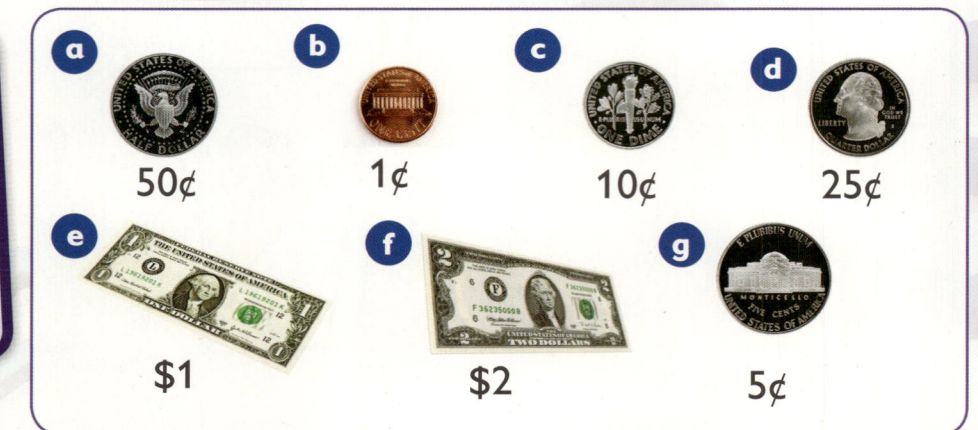

a 50¢   b 1¢   c 10¢   d 25¢
e $1   f $2   g 5¢

**2** Do the math.

1. 🪙 + 🪙 + 🪙 + 🪙 = 86¢
2. 🪙 + 🪙 + 🪙 + 🪙 = ?
3. 🪙 + 🪙 + 🪙 + 🪙 = ?
4. 🪙 − 🪙 − 🪙 − 🪙 = ?
5. 🪙 − 🪙 − 🪙 − 🪙 = ?

**LOOK**
$1.75
One dollar and seventy-five cents.

**3** 🎧 14 CD2  Listen and check.

**4** Read, look, and answer.
1. How much money does Peter have?
2. Can he buy the computer game?

Peter wants to buy a book. The price of the book is $5. He has seven 50¢ coins, six 25¢ coins, and three 10¢ coins.

$5

**5** Ask and answer.

How much is the book and the ball?

That's $7, please.

$5

$20

85¢

$15.99

$1.50

$100

$2

$28.99

$75

$12.50

**Project** Make a store. Go shopping.

How much are the pens?

They're 75¢.

Can I have two, please?

That's $1.50, please.

# Review Units 3 and 4

**1** Play the game.

- START
- go to the bus station
- go to the hospital
- go to the library
- go to the market
- go to the amusement park
- go to the supermarket
- go to the sports center
- go to the movie theater
- FINISH

## 2  Listen and choose the correct picture.

1. What does Jack do on Saturday afternoons?

2. What time does Daisy come home from school?

3. What does Paul do after dinner?

4. Where does Vicky catch the bus?

5. Where's John going?

### Quiz!

1. What time does Sally catch the bus to school?
2. How often does James Flunk go swimming?
3. Do Lock and Key get up before ten o'clock?
4. Where do you catch a bus?
5. What must we do in a library?
6. Where are Mrs. Potts and her friend going?

# 5 Stay healthy

**1** Look, think, and answer.
1. Where are Sally and Scott?
2. Who's the doctor?
3. Is Sally hot?
4. Is Scott sick?

a temperature   a cold   a cough   a headache   a toothache   a stomachache

**2** 🎧 Listen and check.

**3** 🎧 Listen and do the actions.

### LOOK
What's the matter?
My stomach hurts.
I have a stomachache.

**4** 🔊 Listen and say the letter.

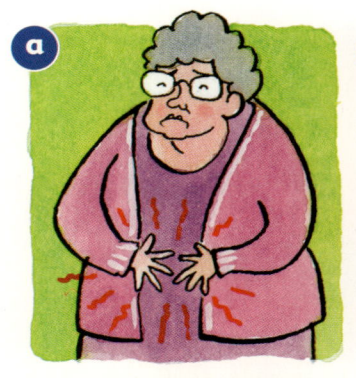

**5** Make sentences. Say the letter.

"She has an earache." d

| He She They | has have | a toothache. a backache. a stomachache. a headache. an earache. a temperature. a cold. a cough. |
|---|---|---|

**6** What's the matter? Act it out.

"My stomach hurts."

"Yes. You have a stomachache."

**7** Look, think, and answer.
1 Where's Sally?
2 Who's Mrs. Star talking to?
3 What's the matter with Sally?
4 Can she go to school?

**8** 🎧 19 CD2 Listen and check.

**9** Complete the sentences.

- Sally must stay in bed.
- Sally must not get up.
- Sally must ...
- Sally must not ...

**LOOK**
We **must not** eat candy before lunch.

48

**10** Read the story. Look at the pictures. Write the correct word next to numbers 1–6.

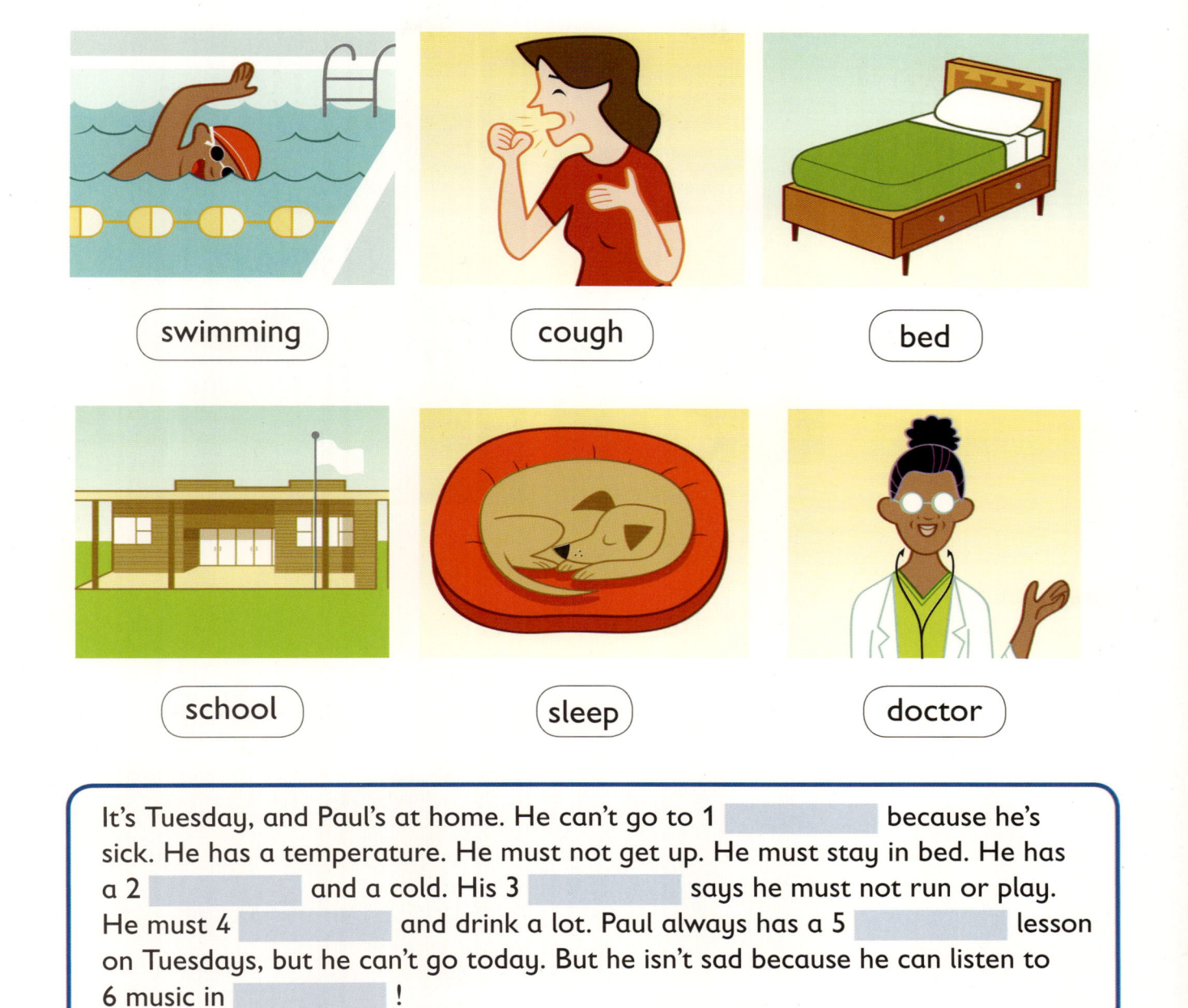

swimming    cough    bed

school    sleep    doctor

It's Tuesday, and Paul's at home. He can't go to 1 _____ because he's sick. He has a temperature. He must not get up. He must stay in bed. He has a 2 _____ and a cold. His 3 _____ says he must not run or play. He must 4 _____ and drink a lot. Paul always has a 5 _____ lesson on Tuesdays, but he can't go today. But he isn't sad because he can listen to 6 music in _____ !

**11** Listen and complete the sentences. Say "must" or "must not."

When you have a cough, you … go out.    … must not …

When you have a headache, you … go to bed.    … must …

49

## 12 Sally's phonics

Sue is at the zoo.

There's a bear on a chair …

and a snake with a toothache!

## 13 Say and answer "true" or "false."

We must brush our teeth with toothpaste after breakfast.

True.

We must not do our homework.

False.

24
CD2
LOCK & KEY
I'm having a big party, and I need some detectives to take care of my beautiful painting, "The Toothache."
No problem, Miss Rich.
This is my beautiful painting.
Ooh, there is a lot of cake!
There's lemon cake, chocolate cake, apple cake, and carrot cake.
Would you like a piece of cake, Sir?
Um ... , I can't choose. Oooh ... Which cake?
I'd like lemon cake, please. Which cake would you like, Key?
Look. I have apple cake, I have carrot cake, I have lemon cake, and I have chocolate cake.
Oh, Key. That's not good for you.
Hmm, what's the matter, Key?
I have some chocolate cake, and now I have a stomachache, too.
... and I don't have my beautiful painting!

## Science — A healthy body

**Fact:** Giraffes only need to sleep 30 minutes every night.

**1** Read, look, and answer.
What's healthy? What's unhealthy?

a. eating a lot of candy
b. running in the park
c. eating vegetables

**2** Read and check. Match.

Sleep and rest   Exercise   Healthy eating

**1** _____
For a healthy body, it's very important to eat the right food. We need to eat different kinds of fruit and vegetables every day. Drinking water is good for us, and we need to drink a lot of it every day. Cake and candy can be bad for our teeth.

**2** _____
Exercise is good for our bodies. We can run and swim or play sports like basketball and tennis. It's important to move our bodies to be healthy.

**3** _____
Our bodies need rest, too. Everyone needs to sleep, and children need to sleep about 10 hours every night.

**3** Quiz

1. What must we eat to be healthy?
2. Name three things we must not eat a lot of.
3. What must we drink to be healthy?
4. How many hours must children sleep a night?
5. What can we do to exercise? Name three things.

4 🎧 **Listen and move.**

swim

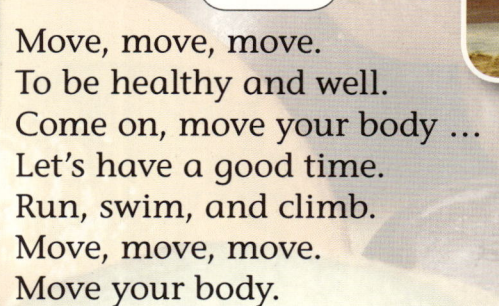

jump

skip

climb

hop

Move, move, move.
To be healthy and well.
Come on, move your body …
Let's have a good time.
Run, swim, and climb.
Move, move, move.
Move your body.

Dance, dance, dance.
Don't stop until you drop.
Come on, you know it's fun.
Dance, dance, dance.
Hop, skip, and jump.
Come on, you know it's fun
Let's have a good time …

dance

run

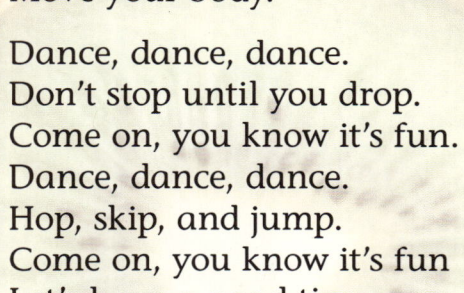

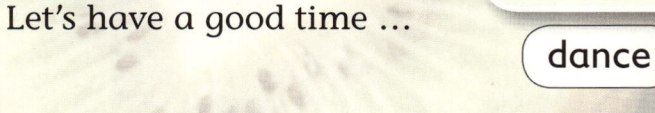

5 🎧 **Sing the song.**

**Project**   Make a "Stay healthy" book.

53

# 6 A day in the country

**1** Look, think, and answer.
1. Where do they want to go?
2. Does Mr. Star want to play badminton?
3. What does Scott want to do?
4. What does Sally want to do?

grass  picnic  leaf  plant  field  river  lake  forest

**2** Listen and check.

**3** Listen and say the letter.

a    b    c    d
e    f    g    h

## 4 Read and complete.

Lily and her brother Charlie enjoy having picnics in the country. Today they're having a picnic in the forest with their grandmother. Lily and her grandmother are sitting on the blanket. They're putting the picnic food on it. After lunch Lily wants to do her homework. She must look at the plants and draw their leaves. Lily's looking at the bread because it's very old and they can't eat it for lunch. Charlie's standing next to the lake. He's throwing bread to the ducks. It isn't the bread for the ducks, it's the new bread for their picnic. The ducks are eating the family's lunch!

1 Lily and her grandmother are sitting …
2 Lily wants to …
3 Lily must look at …
4 Lily's looking at the bread because …
5 Charlie's standing …
6 The ducks are eating …

> Lily and her grandmother are sitting on the blanket.

## 5 Complete the story.

Lily's in the  forest . Lily must look at the plants and draw their leaves. Lily and _____ _____ are putting food on the _____. They're having a _____. Lily's looking at the bread because it's _____, so they can't _____ it. Next to the _____, Charlie is throwing bread to the _____. It's the nice new bread for the family's _____ !

**6** Look, think, and answer.
1. Who's cold?
2. What's Grandma drawing?
3. Where's Grandpa?
4. Where are the cows?

weak
thin
quiet
thirsty
hot
strong
fat
hungry
loud
tired
cold
bad

**7** 🔊 29 CD2  Listen and check.

**8** 🔊 30 CD2  Close your books. Listen and answer.

**LOOK**

**Should** I help you put the blanket on the grass?

56

## 9. Read and complete. Listen and check.

| bad | hair | long | quiet | tall | thin |

People, people here or there.
People, people everywhere.
Different colors, different skin,
Bodies that are fat, bodies that are _____
Some are weak, some are strong
With hair that's short, or hair that's _____
Straight, curly, dark, or fair
Different people, different _____
People, different people, different,
Hungry, thirsty, happy, or sad,
Young or old, good or _____
People are big, people are small
People are short, people are _____
People, different people, different,
Funny, naughty, angry, or tired
Smart, beautiful, loud, or _____
People, people here or there.
People, people everywhere.

## 10. Sing the song.

## 11. Listen and write. Match the words and the pictures.

1 A-N-G-R-Y     Angry – e

a   b   c   d
e   f   g   h

## 12 Sally's phonics

Jen with bread on her head.

Pete with peas on his feet.

Pete and Jen are ready to eat.

## 13 Ask and answer. Use the words in the boxes.

| dirty   thirsty   hungry |
| tired   hot   cold |

| clean   a chair   a blanket |
| an apple   open   a drink |

a. The board's dirty. Should I clean it?

b.

c.

d.

e.

f.

# LOCK & KEY

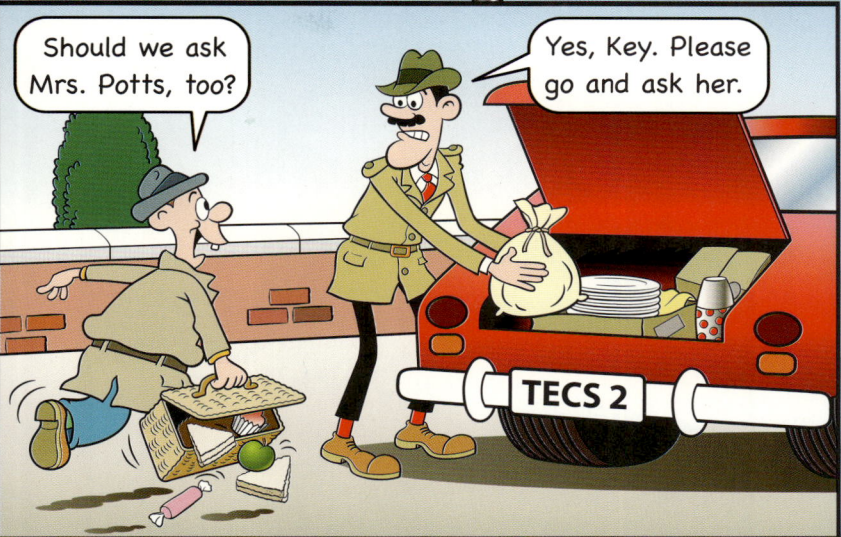

**Let's go out to the country for a picnic, Key.**

**Great idea, Lock!**

**Should we ask Mrs. Potts, too?**

**Yes, Key. Please go and ask her.**

**Should I take a picture of you, Mrs. Potts? Go and stand in front of our car.**

**No, thank you, Mr. Key. I can take one of the lake.**

**Are you hungry, Lock? Should I go to the river and catch some fish to eat?**

**Don't be silly, Key. We have a big picnic.**

**Are you cold, Mrs. Potts? Should I put this blanket on you?**

**No, thank you. It's hot. I don't need a blanket.**

**Well, I can't get you food or a blanket, and I can't help you ... No problem, I can go for a long walk up the mountain.**

**Yes, Key!**

**Good idea!**

59

# Science  Plants

**Fact**
Sunflowers turn their heads to catch the sun.

**1** Say the parts of the plants.

- leaves
- fruit
- roots
- seeds

a. lettuce
b. carrots
c. orange tree
d. sunflower

Plants give us a lot of things to eat. We can eat the seeds, the leaves, the fruit, and the roots of plants.

**2** 🎧 Listen. Say "roots," "leaves," "seeds," or "fruit."

1 – roots

1.
2.
3.
4.
5.
6.

60

3. Ask and answer.

leaves   seeds   roots   fruit

Do people eat the leaves of carrots?

No, they eat the roots.

4. Read, look, and answer.

People need food to eat, water to drink, and air (oxygen). Plants need the sun, air (carbon dioxide), and food to grow. Plants get their food from things in the ground. We water plants to help them grow.

carbon dioxide
oxygen

Which plant is healthy?
What do the other plants need?

1  
2 
3

**Project**   Grow a plant.

# Review Units 5 and 6

**1** Play the game.

Let's take a walk in the country.

**START**

1, 2

3. You must not swim in the lake. Go back 2.

4

5. You can cross the bridge. Go forward 2.

6. Your feet are wet. Go back 2.

7

8. It's dark. You must go forward 1.

9

10. You must throw a six to climb the mountain and continue.

11

12. You can walk in this field. Go forward 2.

13, 14

15. There's a forest. You must miss a turn.

16, 17

18. You can't find your hat. Go back 2.

19

20. You want to go home. Throw again.

21, 22, 23

24

25. You can see the car. Go forward 1.

26. You stop and take a picture. Go back 3.

**FINISH**

**2** Find eight more differences.

In picture 1, there are two oranges. In picture 2, there's one orange.

**3** Choose the right words.

| chocolate | a field | a river | a headache | a picnic | a temperature | a blanket |

1 Cows and sheep sometimes live here.
2 Fish can swim here.
3 This is when your head hurts.
4 Charlie has a toothache. He must not eat this.
5 You have this when you aren't well and you're very hot.
6 You put this on your bed when you're cold.

**Quiz!**

1 Why does Sally go to the doctor?
2 What's the matter with Paul?
3 What's Miss Rich's beautiful painting called?
4 What are Lily and her family doing in the forest?
5 Is Suzy hungry or thirsty?
6 Where do Lock and Key go for a picnic?

63

# 7 World of animals

**1** Look, think, and answer.
1. What are Scott and Sally doing?
2. What animals do you think Sally likes?
3. Which animals are strong?
4. Which animals talk a lot?

Animals of the world

bear, whale, panda, bat, lion, kangaroo, parrot, dolphin, shark

**2** 🎧 Listen and check.

**3** 🎧 Look and complete. Listen and check.

## 4  Read and match.

| a | b | c | d | e |
| f | g | h | i | j |

1  This huge gray animal lives in the ocean. It has a very big mouth and a lot of teeth. It can sometimes eat people.
2  This gray animal lives in the ocean. It has a long nose and small teeth. It's very smart, and it likes playing.
3  This big brown animal lives in Australia. It has two long, strong legs and two short, thin arms. It can jump.
4  This animal can fly. It eats fruit. It can be red, green, and blue, and it's very loud.
5  This big animal is gray, brown, or white. It's big, and it can stand on two legs. It eats fish, meat, fruit, and plants. It sleeps when it's cold.
6  This big black and white bird can swim, but it can't fly. It lives in very cold water, and it eats fish.

## 5  Play the game.

This big black and white bird can swim, but it can't fly.

It's a penguin.

## 6  Read and complete.

huge   eats   cold   sometimes   gray   ocean   animals

This _____ blue or _____ animal lives in the _____. It likes very _____ water. It _____ a lot of small sea _____ and plants. It's _____ very long.

**7** Look, think, and answer.
1. Who's looking at animals on the Internet?
2. Is the elephant clean or dirty?
3. What can elephants carry?
4. Can elephants swim?

**8** 🔊 Listen and check.

**9** What do you think? Read and say "yes" or "no."
1. Whales are bigger than penguins.
2. Dolphins are longer than whales.
3. Pandas are quicker than bears.
4. Bats are dirtier than parrots.
5. Monkeys are better at climbing than pandas.
6. Sharks are worse at swimming than kangaroos.

**LOOK**

| | |
|---|---|
| clean | **cleaner** |
| big | **bigger** |
| dirty | **dirtier** |
| good | **better** |
| bad | **worse** |

**10** 🔊 Listen and complete. Sing the song.

> bigger  see  me  hiding
> snake  smaller  can  than

I'm walking,
I'm walking.
What can I see? …
I can see a lion, and it's _____ than me.

I'm swimming,
I'm swimming.
What can I see? …
I _____ see a shark, and it's uglier _____ me.

I'm standing,
I'm standing.
What can I see? …

I can see a _____, and it's thinner than me.
I'm hiding,
I'm _____.
What can I see? …
I can see a bat, and it's _____ than me.

I'm sitting,
I'm sitting.
What can I see? …
I can _____ a monkey, and it's naughtier than _____.

**11** Make sentences. Use the words in the boxes.

> The cat's weaker than the lion.

quiet
strong
weak

long
big

fat
slow

bad
good

67

## 12 Sally's phonics

A dolphin on the phone.

An elephant with his phone.

The elephant's taking a picture of the dolphin with his phone.

## 13 Read and listen. Complete the text.

Hippos and …

… elephants are both …

# LOCK & KEY

It's Thursday morning. Lock and Key are in their office. It's hot. They're tired and thirsty.

**Hmm ... Robin Motors, the car thief.**

WANTED ROBIN MOTORS the CAR THIEF

**I need a cold drink. Should we stop?**

**Yes, let's go to that new café downtown.**

**Don't look, Key, but Robin Motors is sitting at the table next to us.**

**No, that man's uglier than Robin Motors. His nose is bigger, and his hair's longer.**

**Shh! Be quiet, Key. He can hear you, and he's looking at us.**

**That's not him, Lock. He's the wrong man. Robin Motors is thinner and taller than him.**

**Shh, Key! Everybody can hear you!**

**But he isn't Robin Motors!**

**Oh, yes, he is, and ...HE'S TAKING OUR CAR!**

69

## Geography — Animal habitats

**Fact:** There are 264 types of monkeys in the world.

**1** Read and choose the best name for the text.

> Animal habitats   An interesting picture   Naughty animals

island

A habitat is a place where animals and plants live. Let's look at the habitats on this island. Here there are waterfalls, mountains, and caves under the ground. A big jungle grows in one part of the island. Monkeys, snakes, parrots, and other animals live there. Monkeys and parrots live in trees, and snakes live on the ground under rocks, but sometimes they climb up trees, too.

mountain

cave

waterfall

jungle

**2** Read and match.

> a jungle   a cave   a waterfall   an island   a mountain

1. You can climb it. Sometimes you can see snow on the top of it.
2. It's sometimes under the ground and has a river or a lake in it. It's dark inside, and bats sometimes live in it.
3. It's very hot and wet here. There are a lot of trees and plants.
4. It's a place with the ocean all around it.
5. It's a place where water from a river comes down onto rocks or into a lake.

**3** Look at the animals. What do you think? Ask and answer.

tomato frog

ring-tailed lemur

Nile crocodile

1  Which animal lives in caves?
2  Which animal lives in the trees in the jungle?
3  Which animal lives in the mountains?
4  Why are crocodiles brown?
5  Why do lemurs have tails?
6  Why are tomato frogs red?

**4** Listen and check.

**Project** Make an animal information page.

# 8 Weather report

**1** Look, think, and answer.

1. Who has a pet?
2. Where's Eva on vacation?
3. Who's on vacation in the country?
4. Where's Robert on vacation?

Dear Eva,
We're on vacation in the country. It's windy, and we can fly our kites. It's very wet, too. It's raining now. It rains every day here!
Scott and Sally

Dear Scott,
I'm on vacation at the beach. It's hot and sunny!
Robert

Dear Sally,
I'm on vacation in the mountains. It's great! It's cold and there's a lot of snow. Look at my snowman!
Eva

Dear Grandma and Grandpa,
We're on vacation at the lakes with Dotty. It's cloudy, but I can see a rainbow! It's really beautiful.
Suzy

**2** Read and check.

**3** Listen and say "yes" or "no."

4  Listen and match.     1 – b

a   b   c   d   e   f

5  Ask and answer. Use the words in the box.

What's the weather like at the beach?     It's windy.

cloudy   raining   snowing   sunny   wet   windy   dry

73

**6** Look, think, and answer.
1 Who's Alex talking to?
2 Who's Alex with?
3 Where's Alex today?
4 Is the weather cold today?

yesterday

today

**7** 🎧 Listen and check.

**8** 🎧 Listen and say "yesterday" or "today."

> **LOOK**
> It **was** wet and windy **yesterday**.   It**'s** hot and sunny **today**.
> They **were** out **yesterday**.   They **are** at home **today**.

**9** 🎧 **Read and complete. Then listen and check.**

> coat   cold   hat   scarf   snow   sweater   windy

🎩 , coat, sweater, and scarf,
It was cold and 🍃 in the park, cold and windy …
It was gray and cloudy,
There wasn't any sun,
There weren't many children, it wasn't much fun.
Hat, 🧥 , sweater, and scarf,
It was ❄️ and windy in the park, cold and windy …
There wasn't a rainbow,
There wasn't any ❄️ , 
Grandpa and I were ready to go.
Hat, coat, sweater, and 🧣 , 
It was cold and windy in the park, cold and windy …
Back at home,
It was much better,
With a hot drink and my big red 🧥 . 
🎩 , coat, sweater, and scarf, 
It was cold and 🍃 in the park, cold and windy …
Windy in the park …

**10** 🎧 **Sing the song.**

**11** **Make sentences.**   *It was hot and sunny. She was in a T-shirt.*

> sunny   rainy   snowy   dry   wet   hot   cold   T-shirt   coat   sweater   hat   scarf

**1** **2**  **3**    **a**  **b**  **c**

## 12 Sally's phonics

Why are the whales waiting?

They're waiting for the woman with the watermelons!

## 13 Make a quiz. Ask and answer.

What color was door number 85 on page 21?

It was black.

1. What color was door number 85 on page 21?
2. Where were Lock and Key on page 23?

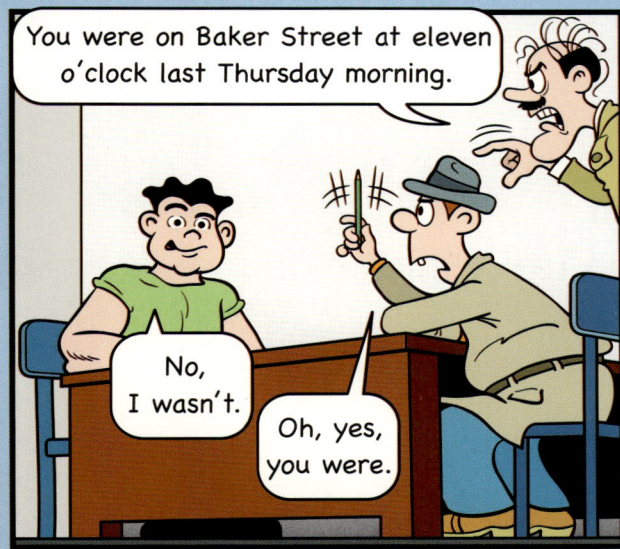

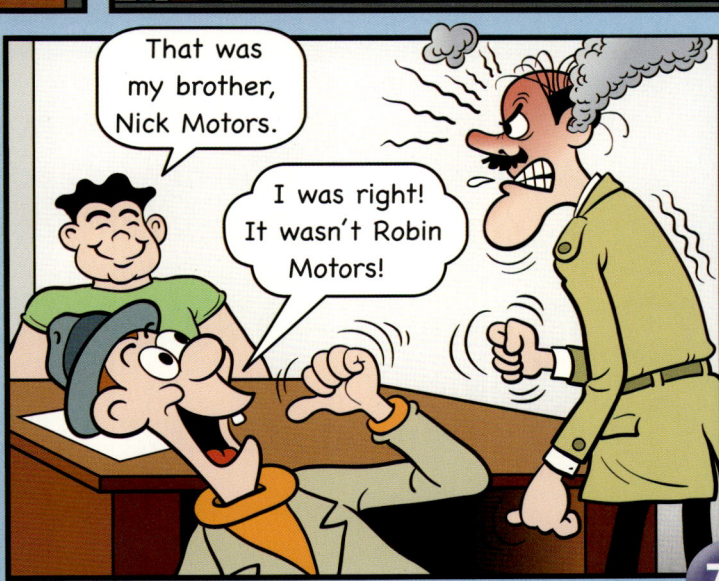

# LOCK & KEY

**Key!** The police have Robin Motors! Let's go to the police station to ask him some questions.

I don't think it was him, Lock.

Are you cold, Lock? No problem. We can go in the car.

But we don't have a car now ... and it's raining!

So, Mr. Motors. Where were you last Thursday morning?

Thursday morning? At what time?

At eleven o'clock.

You were on Baker Street at eleven o'clock last Thursday morning.

No, I wasn't.

Oh, yes, you were.

YOU WERE IN MY CAR LAST THURSDAY MORNING!

No, Mr. Lock ... He was here at the police station.

That was my brother, Nick Motors.

I was right! It wasn't Robin Motors!

77

# Music Instruments

**Fact:** Woodwind instruments can be made of wood, metal, or plastic.

**1** Look, read, and answer.

An orchestra is a big group of musicians. Musicians are people who play different musical instruments. There are four different "families" of musical instruments in an orchestra. These four families are called brass, woodwinds, strings, and percussion.

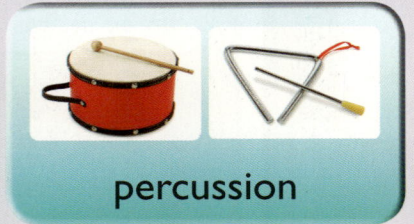

percussion

woodwinds

orchestra

brass

strings

1 Which kind of instruments do you hit and shake?
2 Which kind of instruments do you play with your mouth and hands?
3 Which kind of instruments do you play with a bow?

**2** Listen and check.

**3** Listen. Say "brass," "woodwind," "string," or "percussion."

**4** 🔊 **Listen and say the letter.**
These pieces of music describe the weather.

a
b
c
d

**Project** Make a percussion instrument.

79

# Review Units 7 and 8

**1** Play the game.

### Instructions

1. Groups of four.
2. Choose:
   - weather and clothes
   - animals
   - town
   - country
3. Write words in your notebook.
4. Move and collect your words.
5. Check them in your notebook.
6. Collect seven words!

**2** 🎧 Listen and draw lines. There's one example.

| Daisy | Mary | Sally |

Jack  *f*          Fred          John

### ⏱ Quiz!

1. Which animal sleeps in the day and wakes up at night?
2. Which is bigger, a dolphin or a whale?
3. Where do Lock and Key go for a cold drink?
4. What can you see when it's raining and sunny at the same time?
5. Who was Alex with in the country?
6. Where was Robin Motors last Thursday morning?

# Units 1 & 2 — Values: Give and share

**1** Look and think. Say "yes" or "no."
1. The toys and books are new.
2. Daisy wants to put the books in the trash can.
3. The jacket is too small for Daisy.
4. Jane can wear the jacket.

**2** Listen and check. (CD3, 27)

**3** Read and correct.
1. Daisy's putting books and toys under the bed.
2. The books and toys are for children in the park.
3. The sports center needs books and toys.
4. Jane gives her old books to her grandpa.
5. The jacket is too big for Daisy.
6. Daisy wants to give her jacket to her mom.

**Love your city** — **Values** — **Units 3 & 4**

1. Look and think. Say "yes" or "no."
   1. In the street, it is OK to throw trash on the ground.
   2. In the street, it is OK to write your name on walls.
   3. On the train, it is OK to put your feet up.
   4. In a park, it is OK to play soccer next to the flowers.

2. Listen and check.

3. Read and match.  1 – b
   1. Don't break flowers
   2. You can put your
   3. Don't write your name
   4. On trains and buses don't
   5. In the park don't play
   6. You can help to make your

   a. put your feet up.
   b. and trees in the park.
   c. trash in the trash can.
   d. town clean and beautiful.
   e. on the walls in your town.
   f. soccer close to the flowers.

# Units 5 & 6 Values — Fair play

**1** Look and think. Say "yes" or "no."
1 In sports it isn't always important to win.
2 When you play sports, you don't need to know the rules.
3 In sports you must help other players.
4 It's OK to be angry when we don't win.

**2** Listen and check. (CD3, 31)

**3** Read and correct.
1 We must not be friendly to the other players.
2 You must never follow the rules of the game.
3 When we play sports, it's always important to win.
4 Don't help other players.
5 It isn't important to enjoy playing sports.
6 We must be angry when we don't win.

**Help the world** — **Values** — Units 7 & 8

**1** Look and think. Say "yes" or "no."
1. If you live close to your school, you can sometimes walk there.
2. When you brush your teeth, you can turn the water off.
3. You must not take bags with you when you go shopping.
4. You never need to turn computers or televisions off.

**2** Listen and check.

**3** Read and match.  *1 – d*

1. Turn off the computer
2. Don't always use the car, catch
3. When you brush your teeth,
4. Take bags with you
5. Turn off the lights
6. When you live close to your school,

a. you can walk there.
b. turn off the water.
c. when you go out of the room.
d. when you aren't using it.
e. when you go shopping.
f. a bus or ride a bike.

85

# Grammar reference

| | |
|---|---|
| The doll is next to the ball.<br>The book is on the floor.<br>The bike is in front of the table. | The helicopter is under the table.<br>The game is between the doll and the camera. |

| | |
|---|---|
| What are you doing?<br>What's Daisy doing?<br>What's Peter doing?<br>What are Paul and Jane doing? | I'm riding my bike.<br>She's reading.<br>He's flying a kite.<br>They're playing field hockey. |
| Is Pete flying a kite? | Yes, he is. / No, he isn't. |

**1**

| | |
|---|---|
| Who's Scott?<br>Who's Suzy?<br>Who are Grandma and Grandpa Star? | He's Sally's brother.<br>She's Sally's sister.<br>They're Sally's grandparents. |

| | | |
|---|---|---|
| I | like/love/enjoy<br>don't like/love/enjoy | riding my bike. |
| He/She | likes/loves/enjoys<br>doesn't like/love/enjoy | reading about science. |
| I | want | to ride my bike. |
| He/She | wants | to read about science. |
| Do you like taking pictures?<br>Do you want to take a picture? | | Yes, I do. / No I don't. |
| Does he/she enjoy playing soccer?<br>Does he/she want to play soccer? | | Yes, he/she does. / No, he/she doesn't. |

**2**

| | |
|---|---|
| Does your house have a basement? | My house doesn't have a basement.<br>My house has three bedrooms. |

| | |
|---|---|
| Where's apartment 95?<br>Where's apartment 75? | It's below apartment 85.<br>It's above apartment 85. |

**3**

| | |
|---|---|
| What do you do before school?<br>What does he/she do before school? | I have breakfast.<br>He/She has breakfast. |

| | |
|---|---|
| How often do you play in the park? | I never/sometimes/always play in the park.<br>I play in the park every day. |
| How often does he/she play in the park? | He never/sometimes/always plays in the park.<br>He/She plays in the park every day. |

**4**

| Where do you go to play basketball? | You go to the sports center to play basketball. |

| Must I/Scott/Suzy go to school? | Yes, you/he/she must. |
| Can I/Scott/Suzy go to the swimming pool on Friday? | Yes, you/he/she can. |

**5**

| What's the matter? | I/You/We/They have a headache. He/She has a headache. My head hurts. |

My hand hurts. I can't play the piano.
My foot hurts. I can't play soccer.

He must stay in bed. He must not go to the park.
We must be quiet in the library. We must not eat in the library.

**6**

| I'm hungry. | Should I make breakfast? |
| I'm cold. | Should I close the window? |

**7**

weak → weaker
thin → thinner
naughty → naughtier
good → better
bad → worse

Parrots are weaker than bears.
Dolphins are thinner than whales.
Monkeys are naughtier than lions.
Sharks are better at swimming than elephants.
Pandas are worse at jumping than kangaroos.

**8**

| I/He/She/It | was | at the park yesterday. |
| You/We/They | were | |
| I/He/She/It | wasn't | at the beach yesterday. |
| You/We/They | weren't | |

Where were you/they on Saturday?
Where was he/she/it on Saturday?

| It | was/wasn't | cold and windy yesterday. |
| There | was/wasn't | a lot of snow yesterday. |
| There | were/weren't | a lot of children yesterday. |

# Thanks and Acknowledgments

**Authors' thanks**

Many thanks to everyone at Cambridge University Press and in particular to:

Rosemary Bradley, for overseeing the whole Project and succesfully pulling it all together with good humor.

Camilla Agnew, for her fine editorial skills and tireless dedication to the project.

Karen Elliott for her enthusiasm and creative reworking of the Phonics sections.

A special thanks to all our pupils at Star English, El Palmar, Murcia and especially to our colleague, Jim Kelly, for his help, suggestions, and support at various stages of the project.

**Dedications**

This is for Lydia and Silvia, my own "Star Kids," with all my love – CN
To Pablo & Carlota. This one's for you. Kid's Box's biggest fans. – MT

**The authors and publishers would like to thank the following teachers for their help in reviewing the material and for the invaluable feedback they provided:**

Claudio Almada, Argentina; Sandra Carvalho Araujo, Brazil; Marcelo D'Elia, Brazil; Gustavo Antonio Castro Arenal, Mexico; Rocio Licea Ayala, Mexico; Gilda Castro, Spain; Ana Beatriz Izquierdo Hurbado, Spain; Ruth Mura, Turkey.

**We would also like to thank the following consultants for their invaluable feedback:**

Catherine Johnson-Stefanidou, Pippa Mayfield, Hilary Ratcliff, Amanda Thomas, Melanie Williams.

**We would also like to thank all the teachers who allowed us to observe their classes and who gave up their invaluable time for interviews and focus groups.**

The authors and publishers acknowledge the following sources of copyright material and are grateful for the permissions granted. While every effort has been made, it has not always been possible to identify the sources of all the material used, or to trace the copyright holders. If any omissions are brought to our notice, we will be happy to include the appropriate acknowledgments on reprinting.

**The authors and publishers would like to thank the following for permission to reproduce photographs:**

p.16 (B/G): Shutterstock/Vorobyeva; p.16 (1): Argenteuil, c.1872-5 (oil on canvas) (see also 287548), Monet, Claude (1840-1926) / Musee de l'Orangerie, Paris, France / Giraudon/The Bridgeman Art Library; p.16 (2): Portrait of the artist's son, 1881-82 (oil on canvas) (also see 287554), Cezanne, Paul (1839-1906) / Musee de l'Orangerie, Paris, France / Giraudon / The Bridgeman Art Library; p.16 (a): Alamy/Akademie; p.16 (b): Corbis/Bettmann; p.16 (C): Self Portrait (mixed media), de Villeneuve, Daisy (Contemporary Artist) / Private Collection / The Bridgeman Art Library; p.16 (d): Self Portrait, 1907 (oil on canvas), Picasso, Pablo (1881-1973) / Narodni Galerie, Prague, Czech Republic / Giraudon / The Bridgeman Art Library; p.16 (e): Self portrait, 1889 (oil on canvas), Gogh, Vincent van (1853-90) / Musee d'Orsay, Paris, France / Giraudon / The Bridgeman Art Library; p.17 (a): Courtesy of Hulis Mavruk; p.17 (b): The National Gallery of Art, Washington, Andrew W Mellon fund (John Singleton Copley 1738-1815 / Copley Family 1776-1777 / Photo by Richard Carafellil; p.17 (c): Ursula Roma; p.17 (d): The National Gallery of Art, Washington, Chester Dale Collection (Pablo Picasso 18881-1973/ Family of Saltimbanques 1905 / photo by Bob Grave. G Succession Picasso/ DACs 2008; p.17 (1): Stockbyte/Thinkstock; p.17 (2): Shutterstock/Sanmongkhol; p.17 (3): Shutterstock/Monkey Business Images; p.17 (4): Shutterstock/Monkey Business Images; p.24-25 (B/G): Shutterstock/Lissandra Melo; p.24 (a): Alamy/Greg Balfour Evans; p.24 (b): Shutterstock/Jorge Salcedo; p.24 (c): Shutterstock/Chantal de Bruijne; p.24 (d): Alamy/Stefano Paterna; p.24 (Vicky): Shutterstock/Jaren Jai Wicklund; p.24 (Daisy): Shutterstock/bikeriderlondon; p.24 (Jack): Shutterstock/Monkey Business Images; p.24 (Peter): Shutterstock/bikeriderlondon; p.34-35 (B/G): Shutterstock/zphoto; p.35 (1): Shutterstock/Chirtsova Natalia; p.35 (2): Alamy/imagebroker; p.35 (3): Alamy/Radius Images; p.35 (4): Corbis/ KidStock/ Blend Images; p.35 (5): Shutterstock/Jacek Chabraszewski; p.35 (6): Getty Images/Digital Vison/Photodisc; p.42-43 (B/G): Shutterstock/skvoor; Unit 4, ex. 1 (TL), 2 and 4, p.42: Alamy/© Sam Toren; Unit 4, ex. 1 (TCL) and 2, p.42: Alamy/© JJM Stock Photography; Unit 4, ex. 1 (TCR), 2 and 4, p.42: Alamy/© Sam Toren; Unit 4, ex. 1 (TR), 2 and 4, p.42: Alamy/© Sam Toren; Unit 4, ex. 1 (BL), p.42: Alamy/© incamerastock; Unit 4, ex. 1 (BC), p.42: Alamy/© Carsten Reisinger; Unit 4, ex. 1 (BR), 2 and 4, p.42: Alamy/© Sam Toren; p.42 (boy): Alamy/IndiaPicture; p.42 (game): Alamy/David J. Green; p.43 (jeans): Shutterstock/Mike Degteariov; p.43 (book): Alamy/Ben Molyneux; p.43 (watch); Shutterstock/Venus Angel; p.43 (socks): Shutterstock/kedrov; p.43 (camera): Shutterstock/Masalski Maksim; p.43 (pen): Shutterstock/Raulin; p.43 (football): Shutterstock/irin-k; p.43 (trainers): Shutterstock/Allsop; p.43 (MP3): Shutterstock/Zakharoff; p.43 (t-shirt): Shutterstock/Africa Studio; p.52-53 (B/G): Shutterstock/Sergii Figurnyi; p.52 (silhouettes): Thinkstock/Roman Borodaev; p.52 (C): Alamy/David Grossman; p.52 (a): Thinkstock/Comstock; p.52 (b): Alamy/Lionela Rob; p.52 (c): Shutterstock/AlinaMD; p.53 (skip): Alamy/Juice Images; p.53 (swim): Shutterstock/areeya_ann; p.53 (jump): Alamy/Wildscape; p.53 (climb): Alamy/imagebroker; p.53 (dance): Alamy/Yuri Arcurs; p.53 (run): Alamy/Alan Edwards; p.53 (hop): Alamy/Purestock; p.60-61 (B/G): Shutterstock/danielo; p.60 (lemon tree): Alamy/imagebroker; p.60 (roots): Alamy/leonello calvetti; p.60 (seeds): Thinkstock/Getty Images/Photos.com; p.60 (a): Shutterstock/johnfoto18; p.60 (b): Shutterstock/David P. Smith; p.60 (c): Shutterstock/Georgios Alexandris; p.60 (d): Thinkstock/iStockphoto; p.60 (1): Thinkstock/iStockphoto; p.60 (2): Alamy/mrvee; p.60 (3): Thinkstock/iStockphoto; p.60 (4): Shutterstock/Mazzzur; p.60 (5): Thinkstock/iStockphoto; p.60 (6): Shutterstock/Denis and Yulia Pogostins; p.65 (a): Alamy/Brandon Cole Marine Photography; p.65 (b): Alamy/Holger Ehlers; p.65 (c): Photolibrary.com/Joe McDonald/ Animals Animals; p.65 (d): Getty Images/Oxford Scientific/Daniel J Cox; p.65 (e): Photolibrary.com/Chris and Monique Fallows/Oxford Scientific; p.65 (f): Alamy/Blickwinkel; p.65 (g): Alamy/Bob Elsdale/Eureka; p.65 (h): Alamy/Blickwinkel; p.65 (i): Getty Images/Oxford Scientific/Martyn Ruegner; p.65 (j): Getty Images/Oxford Scientific/Martyn Colbeck; p.66 (L): Getty Images/Hugo Willcox/ Foto Natura/ Minden pictures; p.66 (R): Getty Images/Oxford Scientific/Martyn Colbeck; p.70-71 (B/G): Shutterstock/tobkatrina; p.70 (island): Alamy/Travelscape Images; p.70 (a): Thinkstock/iStockphoto; p.70 (b): Alamy/John Warburton-Lee Photography; p.70 (c): Shutterstock/Patrick Foto; p.70 (d): Alamy/Spectral; p.71 (frog): Superstock/Michael Durham/Minden Pictures; p.71 (lemur): Alamy/Ariadine Van Zandbergen; p.71 (crocodile): Alamy/Ross Warner; p.78-79 (B/G): Shutterstock/Vereshchagin Dmitry; p.78 (orchestra): Corbis/Jacques Sarrat/Sygma; p.78 (brass trumpet): Shutterstock/Mike Flippo; p.78 (brass trombone): Shutterstock/Vereshchagin Dmitry; p.78 (woodwind flute): Shutterstock/Bombaert Patrick; p.78 (woodwind clarinet): Shutterstock/Olga Popova; p.78 (string violin): Shutterstock/Timmary; p.78 (string double bass): Shutterstock/Venus Angel; p.78 (percussion triangle): Shutterstock/Elena Schweitzer; p.78 (percussion drum): Shutterstock/Elena Schweitzer; p.78 (girl flute): Shutterstock/Orhan Cam; p.78 (girl violin): Shutterstock/Martin Novak; p.79 (a): Corbis/Anthony Redpath; p.79 (b): Alamy/Jupiterimages/Comstock; p.79 (c): Alamy/Nigel Cattlin/Holt Studios int Ltd; p.79 (d): Getty Images/Stockbyte.

Commissioned photography on pages 8, 17(B), 19, 25, 34, 35(C), 35(B), 37, 40, 43(B), 47, 50, 53(B), 61, 68, 71(B), 76, 79(B) by Trevor Clifford Photography.

**Key:** T = Top, M= Middle, B = Below, L = Left, R = Right

**The authors and publishers are grateful to the following illustrators:**

Adrian Barclay, c/o Beehive; Bryan Beach c/o Advocate Art; Jenny Nightingale c/o Sylvie Poggio; Trevor Metcalfe c/o Art Agency; Julian Mosedale c/o Beehive; Ken Oliver, c/o Art Agency; Andrew Painter; Mark Ruffle, c/o Beehive; Anthony Rule; Lisa Smith; Mark Turner c/o Beehive; FLP; Laszlo Veres c/o Beehive; FLP; James Walmesley c/o Graham Cameron Illustrations; Gwyneth Williamson c/o Beehive; Sue Woollatt c/o Graham Cameron Illustrations

**The publishers are grateful to the following contributors:**

Louise Edgeworth: picture research and art direction
Wild Apple Design Ltd: page design
Blooberry: additional design
Lon Chan: cover design
Melanie Sharp: cover illustration
John Green and Tim Woolf, TEFL Audio: audio recordings
John Marshall Media, Inc. and Lisa Hutchins: audio recordings for the American English edition
Songs written and produced by Robert Lee, Dib Dib Dub Studios.
For the sound recordings on p 79, Activity 4, track number 25, CD3:
J Strauss Jr - Waltz Op. 410 Voices of Spring. Copyright © Premiere Classics/Getty Images;
Debussy - Estampes: Jardins sous la pluie. Copyright © Premiere Classics/Getty Images;
Richard Strauss - Also Sprach Zarathustra. Copyright © Lee Brooks/Getty Images;
Smetana - My Fatherland: Bohemian Fields and Groves. Copyright © Premiere Classics/Getty Images
hyphen S.A.: publishing management, American English edition